Help For a Child Maltreated While Growing Up: Symptoms, Effects and Preventions

Paul Simon

Table of contents

Chapter 1

Chapter 2

Chapter 3

Chapter 4

Chapter 5

Chapter 1

Treatment

In cases of abuse, treatment can benefit both the parents and the children. The safety and protection of children who have experienced abuse come first. The goal of ongoing therapy is to stop current abuse and lessen its long-term psychological and physical effects.

Health care

If required, assist the child in getting the right medical attention. If a youngster exhibits symptoms of an injury or a change in consciousness, seek emergency medical assistance. It could be necessary to receive follow-up care from a medical professional.

Psychotherapy

Having a conversation with a mental health expert can:

Aid abused children in regaining their trust.

teach a kid about good conduct and interpersonal connections

Improve a child's self-esteem and teach them how to handle conflict

Numerous forms of therapy, including the following:

Cognitive behavioral therapy with an emphasis on trauma (CBT). A child who has experienced abuse can manage their upsetting emotions and memories of the trauma more effectively with the use of trauma-focused CBT. Eventually, the youngster and the supporting parent who has not abused the child are seen together so the child may fully describe what transpired to the parent. parenting and child therapy. The goal of this treatment is to strengthen the bond between parents and children by enhancing their relationship.

Parents can also benefit from psychotherapy:

Learn how to deal effectively with life's inevitable difficulties and the causes of abuse. Learn effective parenting techniques.

Social services may arrange home visits if the child is still living there to ensure basic needs, such as food, are met. Foster children may require counseling or other mental health assistance.

Chapter 2

There are situations when a parent's attitude or behavior raises suspicions of child abuse. Among the warning indicators is a parent who:

shows little regard for the child and doesn't seem to be able to tell when the child is in pain or experiencing emotional discomfort.

Belittles or berates the youngster frequently, calling him or her evil or worthless, among other derogatory phrases.

Expects the child to provide the parent love and attention, and appear envious of the youngster's attention for other family members.

employs strenuous physical punishment

that demands an excessive standard of athletic or academic performance

severely restricts the kid's interaction with other people

and provides no explanation, a contradicting explanation, or an

unsatisfactory explanation for a child's injuries.
repeatedly takes the child to the doctor for examinations or seeks testing, such as X-rays and lab work, for issues that weren't seen during the doctor's examination
a physical penalty

Although child health professionals oppose all forms of violence, some parents nevertheless slap their kids as a means of discipline. While data suggests that spanking is related to worse, not better behavior, parents and other caregivers frequently use physical punishment on their kids to assist them or improve their behavior. It's also connected to issues with mental health, strained parent-child interactions, low self-esteem, and poor academic achievement.
Any physical penalty could cause emotional damage. Even when done in the name of discipline, parental actions that result in

pain, physical harm, or emotional trauma may constitute child abuse.

Relationship Theory

Let's review attachment theory once more. According to attachment theory, newborns scream to communicate their needs. When a baby cries and a calm, controlled caregiver replies, the baby starts to quiet down and gain trust. This bond develops as the trust grows. In contrast, a baby learns that the world is scary and that adults shouldn't be trusted when their needs are not regularly, promptly, or at all, supplied. The baby's emotions, behaviors, and developmental stage will be impacted by this script that is written in their brain.

Cooing and gestures are part of a baby's healthy growth, and parents should respond to them with affection. This beat produces a call-and-response exchange that promotes the child's growth. When this happens, kids feel loved, heard, and seen and they start to believe that the world is a safe place. They start out by writing themselves a script that tells them they are good, wanted, valuable, and lovable. They also think their parents are reliable and trustworthy, and that they will attend to their needs. Since they are more prone to take chances, think critically, and engage others, their developmental trajectory will seem typical.

The World Health Organization claims that 300 million youngsters between the ages of two and four regularly endure physical punishment and/or psychological abuse at the hands of their parents and other adult caregivers. One in five women and one in thirteen males report experiencing sexual assault as a kid between the ages of 0 and 17. 120 million girls and young women under the age of 20 have experienced forced sexual interaction in some way. A country's economic and social development may ultimately be slowed down by the social and occupational effects of child abuse, which include impaired physical and mental health for the rest of one's life. Violence is handed down from one generation to the next because abused children are more likely to abuse others as adults. Therefore, it is essential to stop the cycle of violence and, in doing so, have a good, multigenerational impact. It is feasible to stop child abuse before it occurs, but this requires a multisectoral strategy. Supporting parents, imparting good parenting techniques, and strengthening the law to outlaw corporal punishment are all examples of effective prevention strategies. Care for children and families on-going can lessen the likelihood of abuse repeating and can lessen its effects.

Abuse and neglect of kids under the age of 18 constitute child maltreatment. In the context of a relationship of responsibility, trust, or power, it includes all forms of physical and/or emotional maltreatment, sexual abuse, neglect, carelessness, and commercial or other exploitation that have the actual or potential effect of harming the child's health, survival, development, or dignity.

Chapter 3

The schematization of Child Abuse

There is a lot of overlap and coexistence between various sorts of abuse. The four primary types include

Sexual assault
Violent abuse
Neglect
psychological abuse

Abuse is defined as the deliberate fake, fabricating, or exaggeration of a child's medical complaints to obtain potentially hazardous medical interventions (abuse in a medical setting).

Sexual assault

Sexual abuse is any behavior with a child that is done for an adult's or considerably older child's sexual satisfaction (see

Pedophilic Disorder). Intercourse, which involves oral, anal, or vaginal penetration, molestation, which involves genital contact without intercourse, and forms that don't involve physical contact by the offender, such as exposing the offender's genitalia, showing sexually explicit material to a child, and coercing a child to perform sex acts with other children or to take part in the creation of sexual material, are all examples of sexual abuse.

Sexual play, in which kids of similar ages look at or touch each other's genitalia without using force or coercion, is not considered sexual abuse. State-by-state regulations differ on how to distinguish sexual assault from innocent play, but generally speaking, it is considered unacceptable to have sex with someone who is older than you by more than four years (either chronologically or in terms of mental or physical development).

Violent abuse

A caregiver who physically abuses a child does so by striking them or by acting in a way that puts them in danger. Kid abuse does not always include assault by a person who is not a caregiver or in a position of authority over the child (such as a gunman in a mass shooting at a school). Shaking, falling, striking, biting, and scorching is examples of particular forms (eg, by scalding or touching with cigarettes). The most frequent reason for newborns' severe head injuries is abuse. Abdominal damage is also prevalent in young children.

The developmental stages that infants and toddlers may go through (such as colic, irregular sleep patterns, temper tantrums, and potty training) may frustrate caretakers, making them the most vulnerable. Because kids are unable to report their abuse, this age group is also more vulnerable. In the early years of school, the danger decreases.

Neglect

Failure to address a child's basic physical, emotional, educational, and medical needs constitutes neglect. In contrast to abuse, neglect frequently takes place without any malicious intent.

The various forms of neglect include

Inadequate food, clothing, shelter, supervision, and protection from harm are all examples of physical neglect.

Failure to show affection, love, or other forms of emotional support is known as emotional neglect.

Failure to enroll a child in school, ensure attendance at school, or provide home schooling is referred to as educational neglect.

Medical neglect is the failure to ensure that a kid receives the necessary care or treatment for illnesses or injuries, be they physical or mental.

The absence of preventive care, like as routine dental checkups and vaccines, is typically not regarded as neglect.

psychological abuse

By using words or acts, emotional abuse causes emotional harm. A few examples of specific forms of abuse are yelling or screaming at a child, spurning them by downplaying their talents and accomplishments, frightening and terrifying them with threats, and exploiting or corrupting them by promoting antisocial or criminal activity. When words or acts are ignored or withheld, emotional abuse can also happen, which is known as emotional neglect (eg, ignoring or rejecting children or isolating them from interaction with other children or adults).

Medical setting abuse

When caregivers purposefully induce or fabricate physical or psychological symptoms or signs in a child, it is considered child abuse in a medical setting (previously known as Munchausen syndrome by proxy, now known as factitious disorder imposed on another in the Diagnostic and Statistical Manual of Mental Disorders. To imitate disease, caregivers may administer medications or other harmful substances to the child, or they may contaminate urine samples with bacteria or blood. The exams, testing, and/or therapies given to victims of this kind of child abuse are unneeded, harmful, or have the potential to be harmful.

cultural influences

While severe corporal punishment, such as flogging, burning, and scalding, definitely constitutes physical abuse, different cultures have different definitions of what constitutes abuse when it comes to less severe forms of physical and mental reprimand. Similar to female genital mutilation, some cultural traditions are so harsh they are considered abuse in the US. However, some folk medicines, such as coining, cupping, and irritating poultices, can result in lesions, such as bruises, petechiae, and mild burns, which can make it difficult to distinguish between abuse and acceptable cultural practices.

Symptoms

An abused youngster could experience guilt, shame, or confusion. If the abuser is a parent, another relative, or a close family friend, the child can be reluctant to report the abuse to anybody. It is crucial to keep an eye out for warning signs, such as:

Withdrawal from friends or regular activities; behavioral changes, such as hostility, aggression, or hyperactivity; changes in academic performance; depression, anxiety, or unusual fears; or a sudden loss of confidence; sleep issues and nightmares; frequent absences from school; defiance or rebellious behavior; self-harm or suicide attempts; and

The specific signs and symptoms differ depending on the type of misuse. Remember that cautionary indicators are just that: cautionary. The existence of warning indicators does not imply that a child is being mistreated in all cases.

Sexual abuse signs and symptoms include sexual behavior or knowledge that is inappropriate for the child's age, pregnancy, a sexually transmitted infection, genital or anal pain, bleeding, or injury, and statements by the child that he or she was sexually abused. Physical abuse signs and symptoms include unexplained injuries, such as bruises, broken bones (fractures), or burns, injuries that don't match the given explanation, and burns that aren't compatible with the child's developmental ability.

Chapter 4

Result of Abuse

Abuse has a variety of impacts. There are also sensory pressures, emotional difficulties, and bodily changes. Although the behaviors may seem strange, unexpected, or even excessive, they are actually typical reactions to unusual early childhood experiences.

I heard of a little child who started urinating in shoeboxes and storing the boxes in her wardrobe. Her adoptive parents were attempting to make sense of her eerily peculiar conduct because she had suffered significant trauma at the hands of her birth parents. I reframed it for them after they questioned me about it. She was attempting to determine whether or not her parents were secure and reliable. She was offering them the unpleasant, offensive elements of her to see whether they could manage the heavy pain she carried. She also feared that people would reject her if they saw how great and horrible her suffering was.

They went to her and assured her that they were not afraid of her suffering and that they would always love her. She soon ceased doing this as they gained her trust and sense of security. When parenting a child who has experienced trauma, it is our responsibility to strive to understand their needs. They behave less when we recognize and address their wants.

Developmental Milestones are absent

In contrast, children who endure abuse miss developmental stages and end up with poor self-control, self-regulation, and problem-solving abilities. The narrative they write for themselves states that they are undesirable, unlovable, worthless, and helpless. Adults are perceived by children as being unresponsive, inconsiderate, hurtful, and unreliable. They continue to feel afraid as a result of these ideas, and they question if it is worthwhile to live.

Due to their traumatized pasts, these kids may develop physically different than other kids, putting them at risk for obesity, sickness, disease, and even growth retardation. Their emotional development is also hampered, and they could have a protracted state of worry or anxiety, in addition to having poor physical development. Children who consistently experience fear may lose the ability to distinguish between danger and safety, and they may mistakenly perceive a threat in a benign setting (National Scientific Council on the Developing Child, 2010b).

Some actions might not make sense.

If you ask a child who has experienced abuse to do something or answer a question, you can get an abrupt response or even a meltdown. You'll think that this response just appeared out of nowhere. However, we must react with grace and understanding. They are only attempting to survive the risks, concerns, and anxieties they are encountering; they are not attempting to manipulate us or press our emotions. Because they think the world is dangerous, sometimes their actions seem strange to us.

They have a predisposition to worry and anxiety in addition to a potential for hyperarousal, which can lead to aggressive conduct. These kids might be particularly perceptive to nonverbal signs like eye contact or a touch on the arm, and they might be more susceptible to misreading other people's words or body language.

A Youngster Who Can't Relax

Think of the youngster who is constantly agitated or uncontrollable. Their experience of childhood trauma combined with exposure to violence gave them a tendency to behave violently. Most adults find aggressive actions frightening, and occasionally we want to separate the child or run away from them when what they really need is to be calmed and regulated. They need to understand that we won't turn our backs on them just because they misbehaved. When we distance ourselves from them when kids misbehave, we risk undermining the connection and belonging that they so desperately seek. They don't profit from time-outs since they worry about being left behind. The challenging task of raising a child who has experienced abuse is built on this understanding.

altered brain development

A further effect of abuse is a rise in toxic stress, which affects brain development and limits social interaction. These children or teens experience toxic stress as a result, which may make navigating social situations and adjust to shifting social environments more difficult. They are not at ease. They could interpret others' actions, words, or circumstances incorrectly. Additionally, if they perceived it as a threat, they may respond in ways that are inappropriate for the circumstance.

For instance, when assigned a duty to accomplish, some youth act out by throwing tantrums or shutting down because they fear being abandoned if they fail. Every time he was ordered to take out the trash, one young man would act up. His mother eventually started asking him if she might accompany him as he went to empty the trash. She accompanied him, which helped him overcome his fear (we won't always understand, but we may pray for insight and look for ways to build trust and safety). But we observe this kind of conduct, it can be challenging to react because we want to scold them when what they really need is connection. Before the correction, connect.

Higher Impulsivity

Children who have experienced maltreatment also exhibit higher impulsivity. The child might not be able to solve problems, therefore they behave impulsively and in the present since they are unable to plan ahead. They frequently stay in the present tense. They could also find it difficult at school due to social connections and academic demands. The many sounds, scents, and restrictions in schools can cause sensory overload. Overwhelming events like school or other things might lead to stressed-out emotions and brains. It's critical to acknowledge the difficulties that school presents to our kids and young people.

Other Reactions

Eating disorders, suicidal or homicidal thoughts, violent behavior, inappropriate sexual behavior, discomfort with touch or affection, and high-risk activities are some other reactions to abuse experiences. A child who has experienced sexual abuse may react by acting excessively sexualized. If you observe these actions, try not to become alarmed because they are signs that the child is in discomfort. They want to let go of or release their pain. They could act in ways that are challenging to comprehend or control. Preventing panic and arriving with grace, empathy, and patience is the best reaction we can provide. You might need to join a support group for parents of kids who have experienced trauma so that you can talk about your concerns, bafflement, and pain.

Children under the age of five and those with special needs, such as those with autism, Down syndrome, dyslexia, blindness, or cystic fibrosis impairment, are more likely to experience abuse than typical kids.

A PARENT OR CAREGIVER MAY BE A RISK FACTOR BECAUSE:

Lack of basic parental skills, including failing to set boundaries and being overly controlling as parents, as well as a lack of knowledge and understanding of the child's developmental needs. becoming too protective as a result.

Marital issues, such as disagreements, divorce, and separation

Parenting styles - solitary parenting can be challenging with complicated problems that put the drawbacks of poor money and stress that is connected to lone parenting which increases the likelihood of a parent abusing their child. A youngster who has both parents, on the other hand, is less likely to face abuse and neglect. A father's visible presence and loving role in his child's upbringing and development can benefit the child's cognitive and social development as well as their developmental needs.

Larger Family: Parents with more kids and polygamous families run the danger of abusing and neglecting their kids.

Poor parental attachment, yet "workaholic" parents typically make good providers.

ENVIRONMENTAL AND COMMUNITY FACTORS

There were many dependent youngsters in the family, which caused crowded conditions.

A parent who is experiencing socioeconomic problems, such as low educational attainment, unemployment or low income, substandard housing, or homelessness

REVELATIONS OF RELIGION AND CULTURE

the conviction of demonic spirits

The bond between a child and their parent or caregiver might be harmed by the notion that the youngster is possessed.

The youngster may experience abuse, neglect, or abandonment.

It must be emphasized, nevertheless, that the presence of even one of the aforementioned indicators does not automatically translate into child abuse or neglect, either directly or indirectly. Similar to how protective factors should not be taken at face value, it should not be assumed that a child is protected from all forms of child abuse and neglect or that they are being adequately cared for. This is so that a youngster, even if they are safe and cozy at home, won't be abandoned.

PROTECTIVE ELEMENTS

ensuring that parents or other caregivers are prepared with parental resilience methods to put into practice and establish a long-lasting, secure, and caring environment for the kid they are responsible for, to prevent any type of abuse or neglect.

promote parenting education and the value of protecting children and promoting their healthy development.

Encourage a strong social network

having timely access to necessary resources, such as safe play areas, schools, recreation centers, and health services.

Chapter 5

Guidelines for Preventing Child Abuse

Be a devoted parent.

Children must understand that they are unique, cherished, and capable of pursuing their aspirations.

Support a friend, neighbor, or family member.

Parenting is not simple.
Give a helping hand to look after the kids so the parent(s) may take a break or spend time with one another.

Assisted by you.

Take a break when your daily concerns, both big and small, overwhelm you and make you feel out of control.
Don't lash out at your child.

If your infant wails,

Being frustrated by your baby's crying is normal.
Find out what to do if your child won't stop sobbing.
Never shake a baby; doing so could cause serious harm or even death.

Get active.

Ask your local authorities, clergy, libraries, and schools to create services that cater to the requirements of happy families and healthy children.
Participate in creating parenting materials at your neighborhood library.
Check to see whether your neighborhood library has parenting materials. If not, volunteer to help find some.

Promote school initiatives.

Children can be kept safe by being taught preventative techniques by parents, teachers, and other caregivers.

Keep an eye on your child's usage of the internet, video, and television.

The excessive viewing of violent movies, TV shows, and videos might be harmful to young children.

Participate in a local program to prevent child abuse.

Report any alleged neglect or abuse.

Call the local police or the department of children and family services if you have cause to believe a kid has been or may be harmed.

www.ingramcontent.com/pod-product-compliance
Lightning Source LLC
LaVergne TN
LVHW052111160826
845678LV00015B/3493
* 9 7 9 8 3 5 2 1 9 8 4 3 8 *